DRAGONS
A BOOK OF DESIGNS

MARTY NOBLE

DOVER PUBLICATIONS, INC.
MINEOLA, NEW YORK

Bibliographical Note

Dragons: A Book of Designs is a new work, first published by Dover Publications, Inc., in 2002.

DOVER *Pictorial Archive* SERIES

Library of Congress Cataloging-in-Publication Data

Noble, Marty, 1948-
   Dragons: a book of designs / Marty Noble.
      p. cm—(Dover pictorial archive series)
    ISBN 0-486-42310-7 (pbk.)
    1. Dragons in art. 2. Decoration and ornament—Themes, motives. I. Title. II. Series.

NK1590.D73 N63 2002
745.4—dc21

2002074066

Manufactured in the United States of America
Dover Publications, Inc., 31 East 2nd Street, Mineola, N.Y. 11501

NOTE*

An adequate account of the development of the dragon-legend would represent the history of the expression of mankind's aspirations and fears during the past fifty centuries and more. For the dragon was evolved along with civilization itself. The search for the elixir of life, to turn back the years from old age and confer the boon of immortality, has been the great driving force that compelled men to build up the material and the intellectual fabric of civilization. The dragon-legend is the history of that search which has been preserved by popular tradition: it has grown up and kept pace with the constant struggle to grasp the unattainable goal of men's desires; and the story has been constantly growing in complexity, as new incidents were drawn within its scope and confused with old incidents whose real meaning was forgotten or distorted. . . .

The dragon has been described as "the most venerable symbol employed in ornamental art and the favourite and most highly decorative motif in artistic design." It has been the inspiration of much, if not most, of the world's great literature in every age and clime, and the nucleus around which a wealth of ethical symbolism has accumulated through the ages. The dragon-myth represents also the earliest doctrine or systematic theory of astronomy and meteorology.

*From *The Evolution of the Dragon,* G. Elliot Smith, John Rylands Library at the University Press, London, 1919, pp. 76–77.

1: France (12th century).   2 and 4: France (15th century).   3 and 5: Celtic.

6–9: Heraldry, Western Europe (14th–17th century).

10: Europe (16th century).   11 and 12: France (16th century).

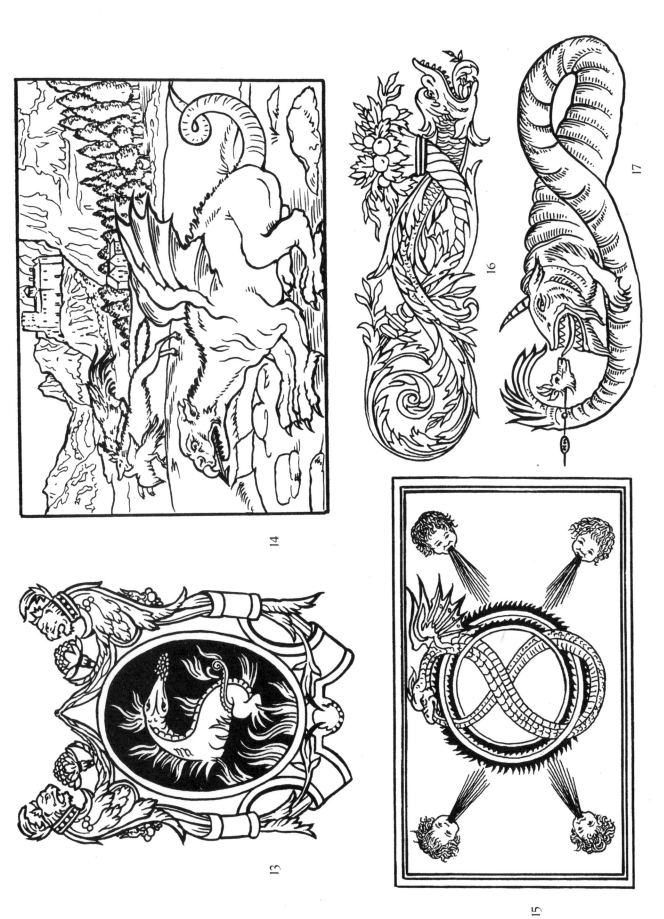

13: France (16th century).   14: Germany (17th century).   15: Italy (17th century).   16. Germany (16th century).   17. Denmark.

7

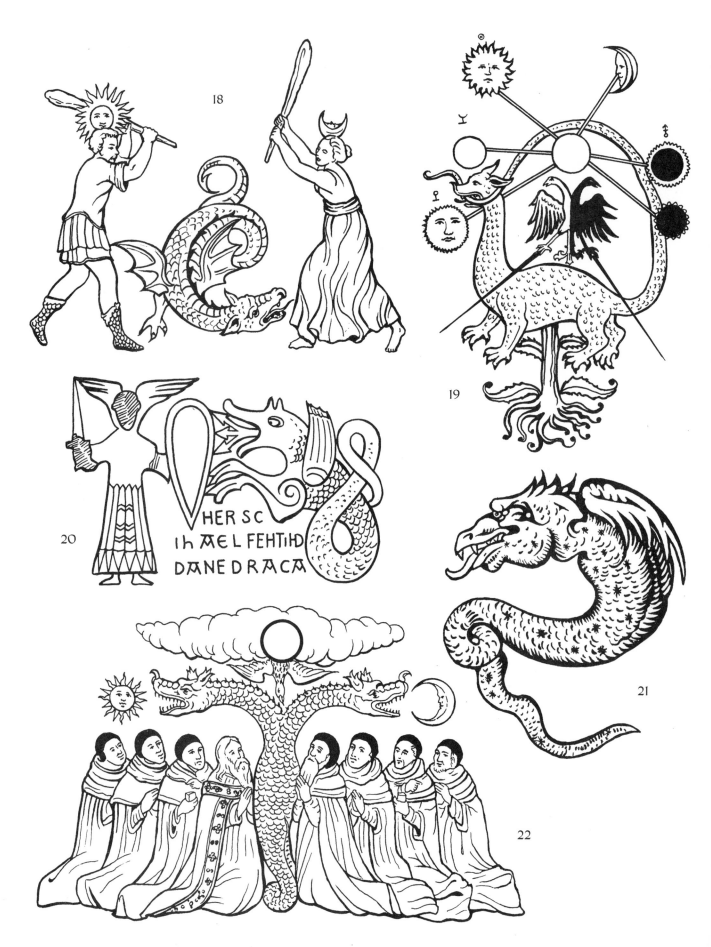

18: Michael Maier, Prague (1617). 19: Germany (16th century). 20: Norman England.
21: European zodiac symbol. 22: England (17th century).

23: England (13th century).   24: Saturn, Babylonia.   25: Europe (17th century).
26: Herbrandt Jamsthaler, Germany (17th century).
27: India (19th century).

28: General.   29: England (late 19th century).   30: William Blake, England (19th century).
31: Michael Maier, Prague (1617).   32: Gustave Doré, France (19th century).

34: England (late 19th century).

33 and 35: Walter Crane, England (1860s).

11

36–40: General.

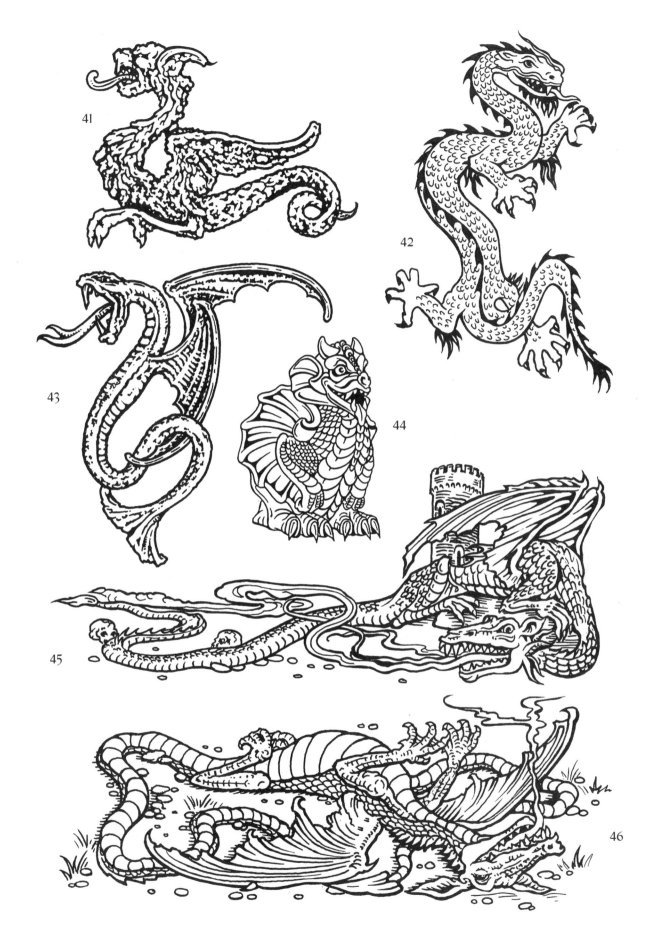

41–44: General.   45 and 46: Walter Crane, England (1860s).

47–50: General.   51. William Blake, England (19th century).

52

53

52–53: General.

54: Italy.   55: Europe (16th century).   56: Brescia, Italy (17th century).
57 and 58: Italy (16th century).

59

62

61

60

59–62: Japan.

63–67: Japan.

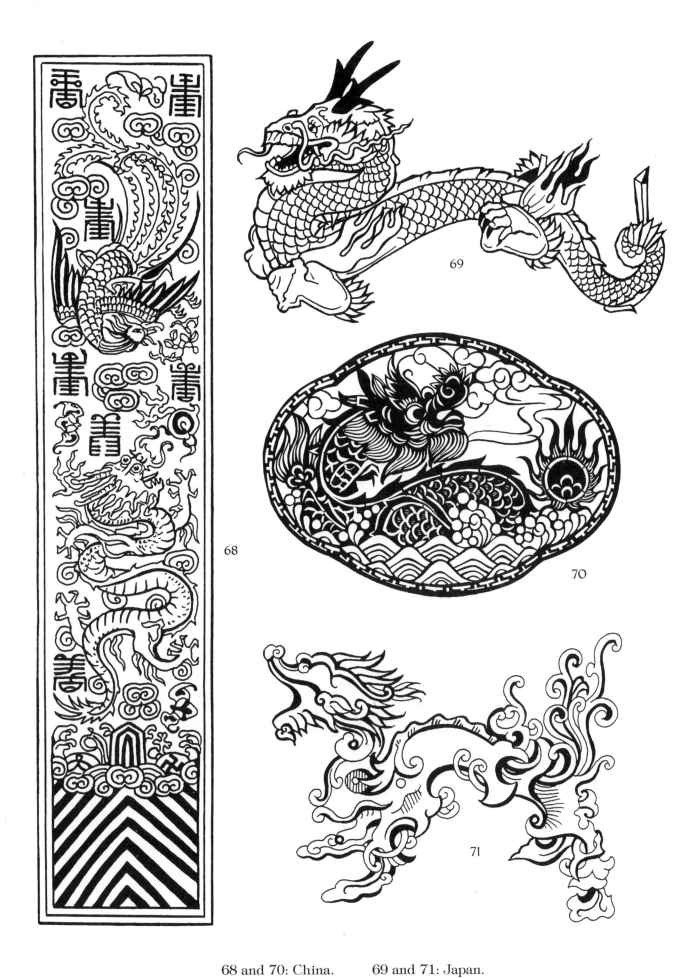

68 and 70: China.   69 and 71: Japan.

72: Greece.   73: Italy.   74 and 76: Java.   75: Indonesia.

77: Babylonia.   78, 80, and 82: Tibet.   79: Sikkim, India.   81: Indonesia.

83: Sufi, Middle East. 84: Bhutan, Himalayas. 85: Greece. 86: China.
87: Tibet. 88: Persia.

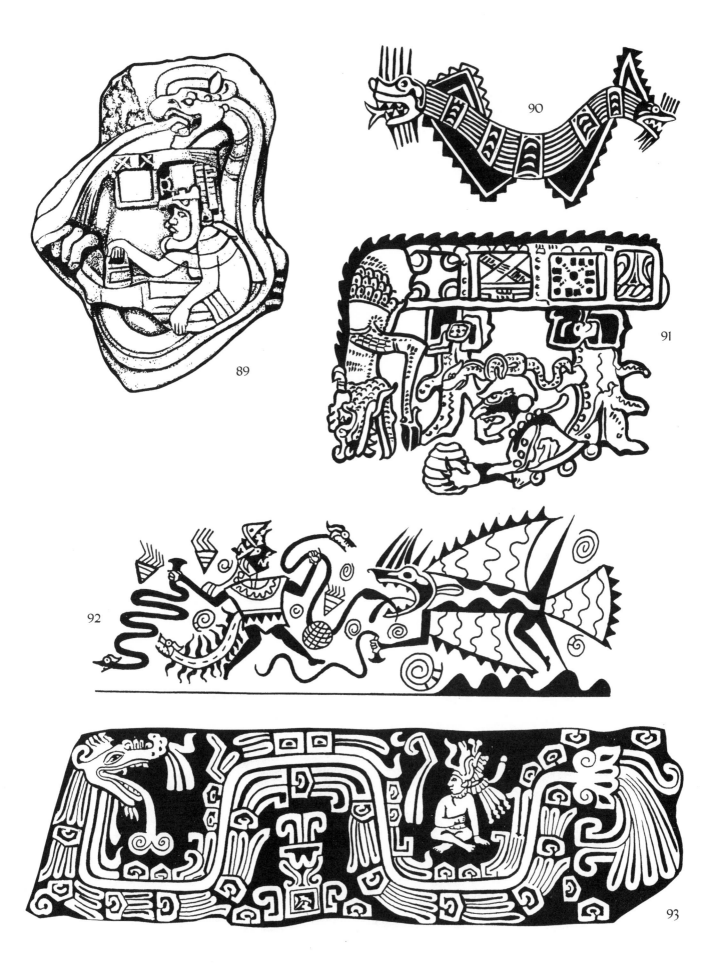

89: Olmec, ancient Mexico.   90: Peru.   91: Mayan civilization, ancient Mexico and
Central America.   92: Peru.   93: Xochicalco, ancient Mesoamerican site.

94

95

96

94 and 96: China.   95: Korea.

97

98

99

97–99: China.

100

101

102

103

104

100–104: China.

105–108: China.

110

109

三

109-111: China.

112–114: China.

115

115: China.

116: China.

116

117–118: China.